the COLLECTOR

Yew

SAGE PRESS

SAGE PRESS,
PO Box Nº 1, Rye, East Sussex TN36 6HN.
e-mail: sagepress.bm@btinternet.com   www.sagepress.co.uk
© Sage Press 1999

Published in 1999
Reprinted in 2001

All rights reserved.

Set in Palatine italic 9 on 11 point leading.
Display in Palatino Light Italic 48 point.

Design and illustrations
Chris Monk of Yellowduck Design & Illustration.

Research
Cindy Stevens

Editor
Cindy Stevens

Series Editor and Publisher
Mrs Bobby Meyer

Printed in Hastings

This book is sold subject to the condition
that it shall not, by way of trade or otherwise,
be lent, re-sold, hired out, or otherwise circulated
without the publisher's prior consent in any form
of binding or cover other than in which it is
published and without a similar condition
including this condition being
imposed on the subsequent purchaser.

ISBN: 0 - 9531644 - 6 - 4

Yew

> "Huge trunks! and each particular trunk a growth
> "Of intertwisted fibres serpentine
> "Upcoiling, and inveterately convolved...."
> (Wordsworth, **Yew Trees**)

Wordsworth's description of yew trees in Borrowdale, Cumbria, could apply to many of these ancient trees in Britain. The yew tree is very long-lived and grows in a particularly convoluted manner which makes it instantly recognisable. Its trunk looks like a cluster of columns because new shoots grow from the base of the bole and then join together. Since it is slow-growing and in leaf during the windiest period of the year, it is often forced into strange shapes by the prevailing winds.

The yew grows wild over most of the British Isles, especially on limestone such as the native woodland on the shores of Lake Killarney. It also grows on chalk downs and Sussex sandstone. Further north, it is found as a lowland tree in some Scottish glens. It tolerates shade well and has been found growing under beech, but little grows under yew itself because of the density of its foliage. In some areas, it has traditional local names such as Hampshire weed or snotty-gogs (a reference to its pinkish-red berries).

Yew also grows wild in other parts of Europe and in Asia, and has been found in mountain areas as far as the Himalayas.

The yew lives to a very great age. There is a saying that it takes '1,000 years to grow, 1,000 to die', but in fact many trees are much older than this. It is difficult to assess their age accurately because the trunk usually becomes hollow after about 500 years, but pieces of the old trunk which have fallen down inside the cavity can be measured and some estimate made from them. It seems clear that many yew trees in Britain are very much older than 2,000 years. Recently, cuttings have been grown from trees estimated to be 4,000 years old.

The yew has associations with religion and legend, has given its name to places, has been used by humans for thousands of years and features in literature. More recently, the native wild tree has been tamed as a garden plant, for hedging and topiary.

Place-names

Yew is a very old tree name, deriving from the Celtic iw (modern Welsh yw). It often appears as a place name attached to isolated dwellings – a recent survey found 74 in Cheshire alone – and sometimes appears in village names. For example, there is a Ewhurst in East Sussex and one in Surrey, and a Ewshott in Hampshire. The Gaelic name for yew – iubhar – appears in place-names such as Inverurie. More modern instances are pub names – there is a Yew Tree at Colwall, near Malvern – and there is an artificially created Yew Tree Tarn fed by a tributary of Yewdale Beck by Coniston Water in the Lake District.

Literature

In his poem Yew Trees, *Wordsworth describes*

>   *"…a Yew-tree, pride of Lorton Vale,*
>   *"Which to this day stands single, in the midst*
>   *"Of its own darkness, as it stood of yore…"*

Another solitary yew featured in poetry is that in Stoke Poges churchyard in Buckinghamshire, under which Thomas Gray is said to have written his famous Elegy. *And Wordsworth also wrote* Lines Left upon a Seat in a Yew-tree, *near Lake Esthwaite in Cumbria:*

"Nay, Traveller! rest. This lonely Yew-tree stands
"Far from all human dwelling..."

In his poem Trees, *Walter de la Mare said*
"Of all the trees in England, Oak, Elder, Elm and Thorn,
"The yew alone burns lamps of peace
"For them that lie forlorn."

And yew berries are used as a symbol in George Meredith's description of the dawn "...that draws athwart the darkness,
"Threading it with colour like yewberries the dew."

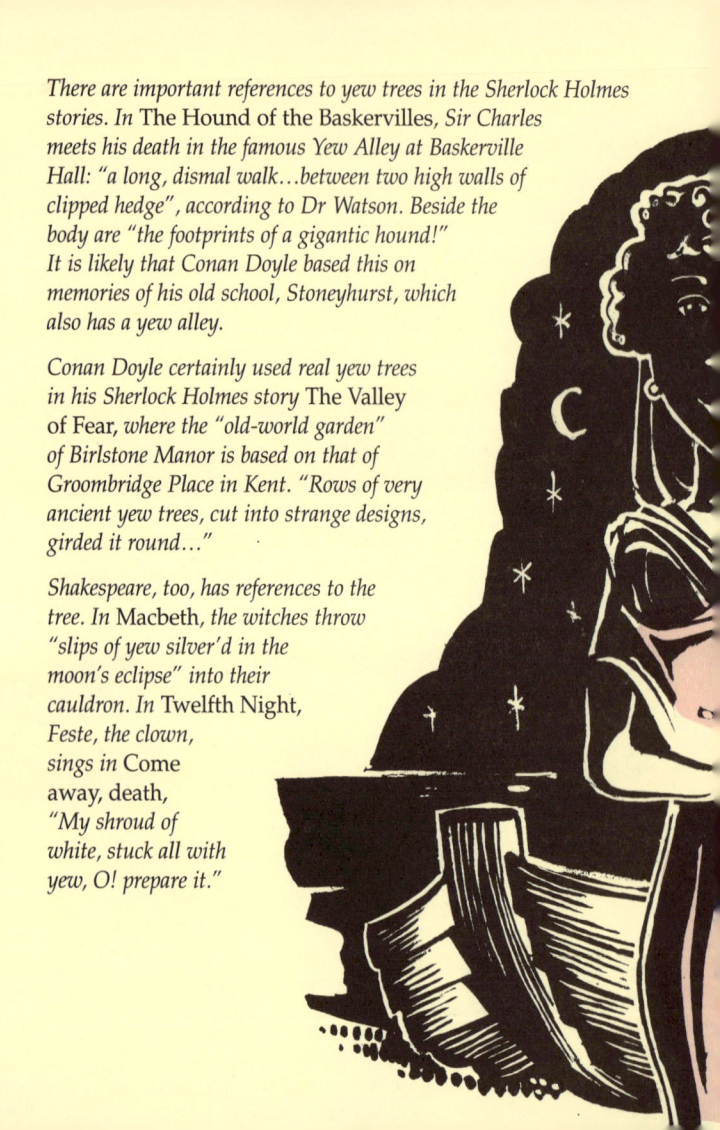

There are important references to yew trees in the Sherlock Holmes stories. In The Hound of the Baskervilles, *Sir Charles meets his death in the famous Yew Alley at Baskerville Hall: "a long, dismal walk…between two high walls of clipped hedge", according to Dr Watson. Beside the body are "the footprints of a gigantic hound!" It is likely that Conan Doyle based this on memories of his old school, Stoneyhurst, which also has a yew alley.*

Conan Doyle certainly used real yew trees in his Sherlock Holmes story The Valley of Fear, *where the "old-world garden" of Birlstone Manor is based on that of Groombridge Place in Kent. "Rows of very ancient yew trees, cut into strange designs, girded it round…"*

Shakespeare, too, has references to the tree. In Macbeth, *the witches throw "slips of yew silver'd in the moon's eclipse" into their cauldron. In* Twelfth Night, *Feste, the clown, sings in* Come away, death, *"My shroud of white, stuck all with yew, O! prepare it."*

Religious and mystical connections

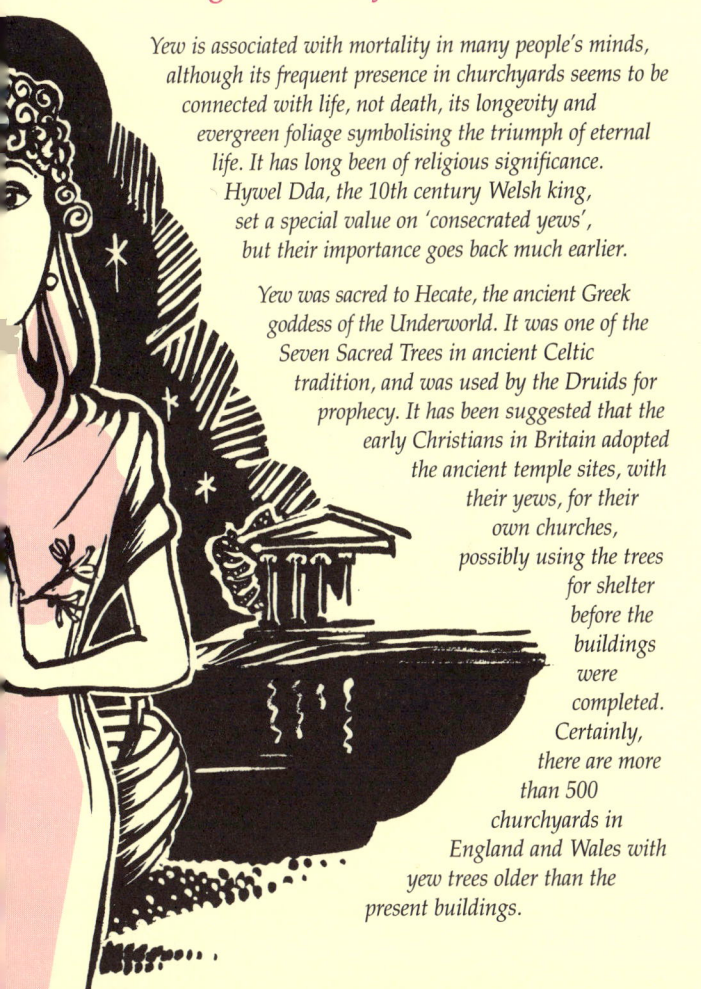

Yew is associated with mortality in many people's minds, although its frequent presence in churchyards seems to be connected with life, not death, its longevity and evergreen foliage symbolising the triumph of eternal life. It has long been of religious significance. Hywel Dda, the 10th century Welsh king, set a special value on 'consecrated yews', but their importance goes back much earlier.

Yew was sacred to Hecate, the ancient Greek goddess of the Underworld. It was one of the Seven Sacred Trees in ancient Celtic tradition, and was used by the Druids for prophecy. It has been suggested that the early Christians in Britain adopted the ancient temple sites, with their yews, for their own churches, possibly using the trees for shelter before the buildings were completed. Certainly, there are more than 500 churchyards in England and Wales with yew trees older than the present buildings.

Yews in churchyards

Most churchyard yews are to be found in south and central England, Wales and the Lake District, owing to soil distribution, but they do grow elsewhere. Legend has it that Pontius Pilate, as a child, played under the tree at Fortingall, Perthshire, when his legionary father was stationed there. Whatever the truth of that story, it seems that the hollow tree was big enough for funeral processions to pass through it in the 18th century.

Many churchyards have yews growing over graves. For example, the ruined church of Llanfihangel Aber Cowyn on the Welsh coast has three graves, 600 years older than the others in the churchyard, which appear to be those of pilgrims going to St David's. When the ancient yew in St Mary's churchyard, Selborne, blew down in 1990, at least thirty shallow graves, the earliest dating from 1200, were found beneath its roots. There is the tomb of a seventh century martyr beside the churchyard yew at Llanafan-fawr, in Powys. More recently, yews were sometimes deliberately planted over graves in order to protect and purify the dead; this could be unnerving for passers-by, according to Robert Turner in Botanologia *(1664), as the branches would draw out the poisonous vapours and give rise to tales of ghosts.*

Churchyard yews may also have a more practical function. In Flora Britannica, *Richard Mabey quotes Susan Cowdy talking about a tree in Buckinghamshire: when it blew down, "the bellringer told me it was very unfortunate for the vergers, etc., as it was always used as a W.C. Its huge, hanging branches concealed all."*

Whatever the origins of churchyard yews, the tradition has been maintained by deliberate planting and protection. In his Natural History of Selborne, *written in the late eighteenth century, Gilbert White refers to a statute passed in 1307 "to prevent the rector from felling trees in the graveyard." At the present day, there is a project to plant 'Yews for the Millennium' in every parish in the country, to ensure their continuation. Each plant will have been propagated from one which was growing 2,000 years ago.*

Yew foliage was used as a substitute for palm branches on Palm Sunday, especially when the festival fell late in the year (if it was early, pussy willow was often used). Some parish records, where there were no yew trees growing in the churchyard, show payment for 'yew palme'. It was also sometimes used as a Christmas decoration.

Uses of yew

Longbows

"The bow was made in England :
"Of true wood, of yew-wood,
"The wood of English bows" (Conan Doyle, Song of the Bow).

"Not loth to furnish weapons for the bands
"Of Umfraville or Percy 'ere they marched
"To Scotland's heaths...'
(Wordsworth, Yew-trees).

Yew is the only tree, apart from the American hedgerow tree osage, to be sufficiently flexible to both bend and return to the straight as required in archery. However, the bow string must always be loosened after use or the bow will set in a curve. The wood is cut from the trunk, not the branches. Medieval longbows were made from a single length and, since yew trunks are often gnarled, suitable wood was much in demand. In fact, much was imported from Spain, careful diplomacy being needed to ensure that supplies were not interrupted in those turbulous times. Spanish and Italian yew tended to be even more flexible than English and was often preferred.

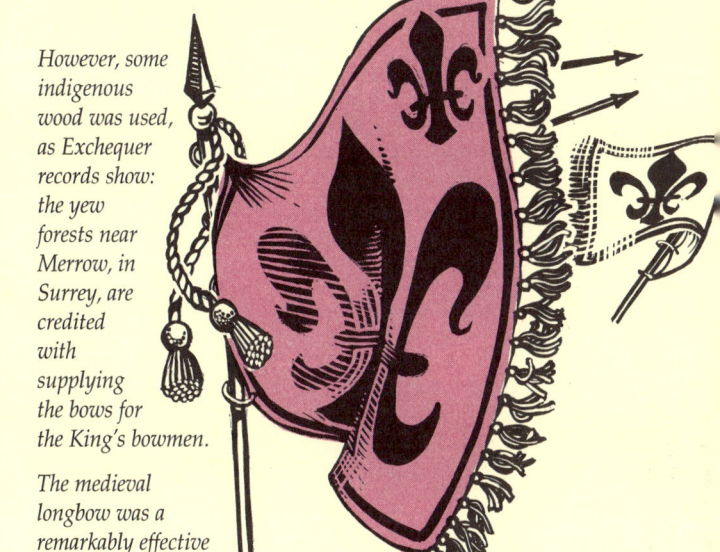

However, some indigenous wood was used, as Exchequer records show: the yew forests near Merrow, in Surrey, are credited with supplying the bows for the King's bowmen.

The medieval longbow was a remarkably effective weapon, eight times quicker to reload than a crossbow, and capable of releasing 100lb pressure each time it was used. 7,000 archers could release 100,000 arrows per minute, and their expertise was vital in battles such as Crécy and Poitiers. The amazing defeat of a large French force by the small, travel-weary army of Henry V at Agincourt can be explained only by the skill of the longbowmen.

The wood for medieval bows was cut so as to have both heartwood, to be put under compression for strength, and sapwood, to be put under tension for flexibility. By Victorian times, bows were made from two lengths of yew spliced together in the middle. Merriden, in Warwickshire, continued to hold an archery competition using medieval-style one-piece bows, or 'self-bows', until well into the 20th century.

Other uses

Yew is one of the heaviest softwoods, being almost as hard as oak. It dries well and relatively quickly, is resistant to splitting and is one of the few softwoods to be able to be steam-bent. In colour, it resembles mahogany, darkening from red to brown with age. It is fine-grained and attractive. With all these attributes, it is no wonder that it has been widely used for centuries.

Yew spears were often used in prehistoric times. One of the oldest known wooden artefacts in the world is a 250,000 year old spear found at Clacton, in Essex. And one was found in Saxony between the ribs of an elephant.

The Vikings used yew knotwood for the nails in their ships. The Bronze Age boats found at North Ferriby on the Humber used yew roots: the fifty foot long boats were made of thick oak beams caulked with moss, held in place with thin oak laths and secured by stitching made from twisted yew roots.

Yew has been used in furniture making, in craft pieces rather than mass production. Steam-bent yew was particularly useful for the hooped backs of Windsor chairs.

Baskets can be woven from the fine branches. Its bast – the fibrous inner part of the bark – can be woven into rope or fabric. The name **Taxus** *is thought to come from the Latin* **texere** *– to weave.*

Other indoor uses were for veneer for panelling, musical instruments, walking sticks and small domestic items. With its fine, uneven grain, it is also used for decorative carved pieces. The dark heartwood and pale sapwood can look very effective together.

Outdoors, the great durability of yew made it ideal for fencing and gateposts, and it was sometimes used for the heavy framework of mills. It was particularly valued before the widespread use of iron, as it is so hard and resists the action of water well.

In recent years, there has been research into the pharmaceutical use of the leaves. The alkaloid, taxol, which is produced from them appears to be useful against ovarian cancer. The religious community at Burford Priory has had a contract to supply a pharmaceutical company with its yew clippings and some private gardeners collect theirs for the same purpose.

Yews provide good shelter. Many isolated farmhouses and other buildings have ancient yews beside them, usually planted against the prevailing winds. Since they are frequently hollow, they have even been used for storage and habitation. There is also some indication that they have been used as marker trees.

The yew was used as a symbol on the old drove roads in the Ashdown Forest in Sussex. A sign showing two yews meant that there was overnight accommodation for drovers, while three yews indicated that there was also accommodation for their animals.

Famous yews

*There is a tree in the churchyard at Crowhurst, East Sussex, which was used, legend claims, to hang King Harold's steward after the Battle of Hastings. His 'crime' was refusing to reveal the whereabouts of the royal treasure. John Aubrey saw the tree in 1680, when its diameter was 2.62m; it had grown to 2.89m by 1998.
Also in Sussex, at Coldwaltham, and at Llanfaredd, in Powys, there are yews which are estimated to be 3,000 years old.*

Older still is a tree in the churchyard at Discoed, also in Powys, near a Bronze Age burial mound. Mentioned in the Domesday Book, it is now estimated to be 5,000 years old.

John Wesley is said to have preached under a yew at High Lorton, in Cumbria.

There is a yew over the site of the ancient holy well at Glangwenlais, near Ammanford, Dyfed.

A tree in Shining Cliff Wood, near Ambergate, Derbyshire, is alleged to have been the inspiration for the nursery rhyme Rock-a-bye Baby. *It was occupied by a family who hollowed out a branch to use as a cradle.*

The monks of Wilmington Priory in Sussex are said to have planted twelve yew trees to represent the Apostles at Ratton Manor, Willingdon. Legend says that they put a curse on anyone who dared to fell them. Although it seems unlikely that the present trees date back to that time, the felling of three of them in the 1960s was followed by the deaths of the owner and two of the tree surgeons involved. The remaining trees are now under a preservation order.

Mazes

Yew makes an ideal plant for a hedge maze, such as the famous one at Hampton Court. In **Three Men in a Boat**, Jerome K. Jerome has an amusing account of how Harris, and all the visitors then in the maze, become hopelessly lost in it. They call for a keeper to help them but "He was a young keeper, as luck would have it, and new to the business; and when he got in, he couldn't get to them, and then he got lost ... They had to wait until one of the old keepers got back from his dinner before they got out."

Hedge, or puzzle, mazes were much in vogue by the end of the 18th century, and most stately homes had them. Longleat House has the largest in the world. They were planted for amusement, unlike the older mazes of turf or stone which often had religious or symbolic significance.

There has been a recent revival of interest in mazes. Leeds Castle, in Kent, has a modern hedge maze, with 2,400 yews having been planted along frames in 1988. Unlike more traditional mazes, it has a separate exit, through an underground labyrinthine grotto. The 19th century hedge maze at Saffron Walden, in Essex, has recently been restored.

Topiary

Yew is a popular plant for topiary; indeed, some gardeners consider it to be the best of all. It is solid in appearance, needs only an annual trim and has small leaves which do not look untidy or go brown after cutting. Vita Sackville-West thought that it should not be used for small pieces of topiary but for 'heavy and sombre archways, or…huge balls and obelisks'.

It is often grown as cones or pillars in formal gardens; Hadleigh Guildhall, in Suffolk, uses a yew gnomon in its sundial garden. Topiary shapes should be of a tapering design so that light can reach all the surfaces and keep the plant healthy.

Yew is often used architecturally instead of walls. "You may almost be said to build with yew hedges" (Christopher Lloyd). A crenellated or buttressed style can be particularly effective because of the dramatic effects of light and shade that may be obtained.

Packwood House in Warwickshire has some remarkable yew topiary. A 17th century owner wanted to illustrate the Sermon on the Mount and used yew cones for the multitude and the apostles. The cones increase in size with their importance and proximity to the mount.

Hedges

Yew is much used for hedging, although not everyone is convinced of its value in smaller gardens. Susan Hill complained of her hedge that "It is dark, it is dead…it never changes, never reflects or lightens, only glowers", yet Christopher Lloyd suggests that a yew hedge will become "truly frivolous" in early summer when the new shoots will vary from plant to plant in shades of pale green or bronze. The individual plants will also vary in vigour and so one can choose to clip along severe lines or allow the hedge to bulge slightly as it will. It also provides a good background for flowers, being generally dark in hue and so making a good contrast.

Apart from yew alleys, yew tunnels have sometimes been planted. Aberglasney, a long-neglected Elizabethan mansion near Llandeilon, Carmarthenshire, has recently had its formal garden restored. Its yew tunnel, shown below, believed to be over 500 years old, is the longest in Britain. When restoration began, it had become so tall during the years of neglect that it overtopped the house.

Cultivation

Yew likes well drained soil and does not grow well in town gardens where there is pollution. It needs good drainage and some experts place tile drains under the hedges when planting. The dangers of over-watering are shown in the replanting of the Selborne churchyard tree after it blew down in January 1990. When it was replanted the following month, a water main burst nearby and ran for 36 hours. This seemed no bad thing at first, and the tree grew new shoots, but it was clearly dead by 1992, most probably of an excess of water.

For hedging, it is best to use small plants, no more than two feet high, with growth all the way up the stems. Trials carried out by Nathaniel Lloyd showed that, after nine years, one foot high plants had reached the same height as those planted at three feet while many of those planted at six feet had been lost. Christopher Lloyd, his son, recommends setting the plants three feet apart ; this will look sparse at first but the mature plants would be starved if put closer together.

Although yew is slow to grow at the beginning, it should take no more than ten years to achieve a mature hedge. In **Creating Small Gardens**, Roy Strong describes making a new hedge from 18 inch plants; it had reached eight feet after twelve years.

Late March or April is the best time for planting, but beware drought.

Cut the plants well back after one year to encourage dense, bushy growth. Yew responds well to hard pruning, although it is probably safest to tackle only one side a year if dealing with a very neglected hedge. For normal maintenance, it should be clipped in August, after which its sharp outline should last until the end of May.

The average gardener is unlikely to have the space to grow a yew tree, as individual specimens should be planted well away from any building: twelve metres is probably the minimum distance desirable. If the site is sheltered, it is possible to use plants as small as one foot high; elsewhere, it is best to grow them on (with frost protection) for a *further 6-12 months. The tree should reach 20 feet after about 50 years; subsequent growth will slow down.*

Whether planting hedges or individual specimens, do as you would for any other plant: heel-in bare-rooted bushes (or wrap them in sacking) if you are unable to plant immediately, and keep the soil moist after planting. The roots can be invasive, making it difficult to have flower beds immediately beyond a hedge unless you take preventative action – Nathaniel Lloyd sank three foot long sheets of galvanised iron into the ground beyond his hedges when he planted them at Great Dixter early this century. Feed regularly – fish, blood and bone in winter is recommended - and remove ivy and other invasive climbers. If you wish to restore badly neglected plants, it is a good idea to feed and mulch them for a year before attempting drastic pruning.

Nonetheless, neglected yew usually responds very well to severe action, with new shoots growing readily from a skeleton of old wood.

The poison debate

Yew is often considered to be a deadly plant but there is a surprising amount of debate about which parts are poisonous. A book on wild plants published in 1938 states that the berries are not poisonous at all, and Gerard, the 16th century herbalist, says that he and his school friends "did eat our fill of the berries of this tree". Certainly birds eat them, especially thrushes and other soft-billed birds in hard weather. Yet more modern books describe the berries as deadly. It seems likely that the dangerous part is the seed, which birds excrete, this being how yew is propagated.

It seems clear that the leaves are poisonous to some creatures. The 1930s edition of an Observer's Pocket Guide to Trees *states that "it appears that though cattle and goats may eat them, often with impunity, horses and humans pay the penalty of death for such indulgence.'" Yet there have been instances of horses, as well as sheep and cattle, eating the fresh lower branches and seedlings without ill-effect, while there are also recorded instances of cattle being poisoned. In some areas, roe deer have grazed the plants almost into topiary shapes without apparent harm to themselves.*

What does seem clear is that withered foliage and clippings are highly dangerous, since they contain a deadly alkaloid which is also present in the seeds and bark.

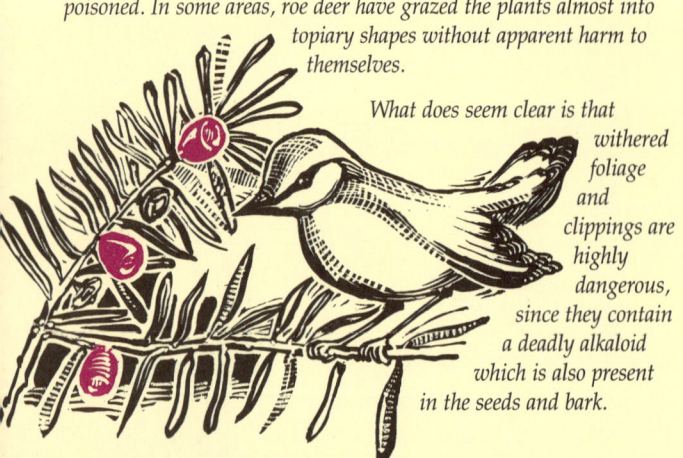

Varieties of yew

The most common form is the wild yew, Taxus baccata, *but other forms are available. Golden yew,* Taxus baccata aurea, *was especially popular in Victorian shrubberies and is a useful plant for creating contrast in topiary designs. Weeping varieties are available.*

The Irish yew, Taxus fastigiata, *has erect branches and looks rather like a Mediterranean cypress or Lombardy poplar. All Irish yew is descended from two plants which were found on the Florence Court estate in County Fermanagh in 1780. There is also a golden variety with variegated leaves.*

The Japanese yew, Taxus cuspidata, *is hardier.* Taxus cuspidata aurescens *is a dwarf form producing golden-yellow shoots in the first year and dark green ones later.*

Yew

"... *a living thing*
"*Produced too slowly ever to decay;*
"*Of form and aspect too magnificent*
"*To be destroyed...*"

(Wordsworth,
Yew-trees)

Botanical Notes

Common name: Yew

Botanical name: Taxus baccata

Family: Taxaceae

Size: 5 to 15 metres in height; girth can exceed 15 metres.

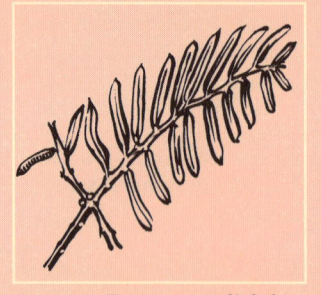

Leaves: Evergreen, slightly curved. Leathery in texture, shiny and dark above, pale and dull underneath.

Branches: Start quite close to the ground, grow almost horizontally, with many leafy twigs.

Trunk: Appears to be several trunks fused together; new shoots grow from the base and coalesce with the old wood.

Bark: Thin, red, flakes off in patches.

Flowers: Male and female grow on separate trees, although occasionally a tree will bear one or two branches with flowers of the opposite sex.

Male: almost round, about $1/2$ cm across, containing about six yellow anthers, the base surrounded by dry overlapping scales. February-March, on the underside of branches. Female: much smaller – one seed-egg standing on a fleshy disc with a few scales at its base.

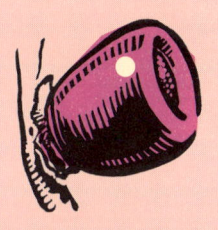

Fruit: Red or pinkish-red berry, open at the top to show the olive-green seed.

In the same series
Ash
Box
Cedar of Lebanon
Hawthorn
Holly
Monkey Puzzle
Oak

To be published in 2002
Caring for Box
Fig
Monkey Puzzle Gazetteer
Willow

To be published soon
Beech
Birch
Catalpa
Elm
Mulberry
Sweet Chestnut

If you enjoyed this and would like to buy
any of the above titles or require
further information
please contact

SAGE PRESS
PO Box Nº 1, Rye, East Sussex TN36 4HN.
e-mail: sagepress.bm@btinternet.com www.sagepress.co.uk